NEW BIRTH
OR REBIRTH?

D0170577

RAVI
ZACHARIAS

MULTNOMAH
BOOKS

NEW BIRTH OR REBIRTH?
PUBLISHED BY MULTNOMAH BOOKS
12265 Oracle Boulevard, Suite 200
Colorado Springs, Colorado 80921
A division of Random House Inc.

ISBN: 978-1-59052-725-2

Published in association with the literary agency of Wolgemuth & Associates Inc.

Library of Congress Cataloging-in-Publication Data
Zacharias, Ravi K.
    New birth or rebirth? : Jesus talks with Krishna / Ravi K. Zacharias. — 1st ed.
    p. cm.
    ISBN 978-1-59052-725-2
    1. Jesus Christ—Fiction. 2. Krishna (Hindu deity)—Fiction. 3. Imaginary conversations. I. Title.
PS3576.A19N49 2008
813'.54—dc22

                                                2007047027

Printed in the United States of America
2008—First Edition

10 9 8 7 6 5 4 3 2 1

Special Sales
Most WaterBrook Multnomah books are available in special quantity discounts when purchased in bulk by corporations, organizations, and special interest groups. Custom imprinting or excerpting can also be done to fit special needs. For information, please e-mail SpecialMarkets@WaterBrookMultnomah.com or call 1-800-603-7051.

INTRODUCTION

Krishna is revered by millions of people worldwide, and writing on any figure honored that greatly is difficult.

But I am doing so because the one notion that all religions subscribe to (either explicitly or implicitly) is the notion of exclusive truth. Populists like to deny that premise, but all religions either make this claim or try to covertly smuggle it in.

The question, therefore, is not whether one enjoys a discussion like the one that follows in this book but whether the arguments are fairly presented. That is much harder to do, especially where length is limited. I have, therefore, selected to write about what I consider to be the greatest differences between Jesus and Krishna.

As always, putting words into the mouths of historic figures is a challenge. I have done my best to take ideas straight from what has already been quoted in each faith's sacred texts and put them into context here.

Hinduism is a complex belief system. At times the following conversation will become quite philosophical and intricate. Please be patient as we work through these areas of belief so that the truth and beauty of Christ's gospel is fairly presented against the backdrop of

Hinduism's complexity. To present either of these beliefs as simple is to not understand them fully.

As with the other books in this series, I have introduced a third personality who can raise questions legitimately, since any known conversations between Jesus and Krishna do not exist.

Subramaniam was a real person. Born a Hindu in the early part of the twentieth century, his is one of the most remarkable stories I have ever read. He challenged the religion of his birth and faced immense persecution for his actions, being ostracized and finally fleeing from his hometown to avoid death.

Incidentally, I have always marveled that so many religions exact this kind of revenge against dissenters. It only weakens the appeal of their own faith and contradicts any claims they might have made that "all religions are basically the same." If all religions are indeed the same, why not let someone be "converted" to another religion?

I also marvel at the fury sometimes evident in those who attack others for examining and questioning their own worldview. If the repercussions of converting weren't so serious, it would almost be comical to see the animosity of the responses.

But what this revenge demonstrates so strongly is an inbuilt belief that conversion is wrong. And why is conversion so forbidden? It circles back again to the one notion that all religions subscribe to—the notion of exclusive truth.

I have also introduced a fourth character, Richard, a fictional traveler to India who converses with Subramaniam on the road to Mathura and later eavesdrops on the conversation between Jesus, Krishna, and

Subramaniam. Richard does not lean heavily behind the curtain, as Subramaniam does, but it is my hope that he will someday—as it is my hope that all people who seek spiritual truth will.

Another factor is at stake in the following discussion: it is easy to take the weakest aspect of a worldview and exploit it. But that is not what I wish to do. When one encounters expressions of belief that are openly affirmed and followed, even when they seem bizarre, one must ask the hardest questions. One must examine the stronger aspects of any worldview as well.

At base, one of my consistent premises throughout this series is that the popular aphorism "All religions are fundamentally the same and only superficially different" simply is not true. It is more correct to say that all religions are, at best, superficially similar but fundamentally different.

In the pages to come, I hope that the vast differences between Christianity and Hinduism will become very evident in this imaginary dialogue. Yet it is important to remember that, as different as these faiths are, we must learn to accept those differences peaceably.

Still, let us not be so mindless as to think that Christianity and Hinduism are saying the same thing and that, in the end, the differences do not really matter. Both claim to be true and legitimate. This rationally implies, then, that it *does* matter what you believe.

That is what this imaginary dialogue is about.

—*Ravi Zacharias*

PROLOGUE

Richard: Subra—*look out!* That car is coming straight at us!

Subramaniam: Relax, my friend. This is how people here drive all the time.

Richard: Ooooh! Here comes another one—watch out! Is that guy drunk or something?

Subra: Just hang on. We will be there shortly.

Richard: I thought this was a divided highway… Where did all these cars come from all of a sudden? There are more coming!

Subra: It *is* a divided highway. I'm sure that guy is just dropping off workers who live on this side of the village. To drive another several kilometers to turn around is a waste of money and time. You see, in England they drive on the left, in America on the right. But here in India we drive in the shade…or wherever else is convenient.

Richard: I don't believe it! I simply don't believe it! This could kill a fellow…

Subra: *[Laughing]* Now you know why we don't need a Disneyland in India. Driving provides all the scary rides we could ever want. What were we talking about a few minutes ago anyway?

Richard: Uh…let me unclench my fists first. You were telling me about your background. It's hard to pray and listen at the same time, but I'll try. Please carry on with what you were saying…

Subra: Ah yes, now I remember. It was the hardest thing I ever did, Richard—to question what was so deeply ingrained in my family's faith. Everything in my family was built around our faith. On the most important day of my childhood, it was hard to see my mother absent from the ceremony.

Richard: *The most important day of your childhood?* I think in such Western terms that I hesitate to even ask what you mean. What day are you talking about? You certainly don't mean the day you were born.

Subra: Well almost, but not quite. Let me explain…

As you know, society in India is built on the caste system. There are four main castes: Brahmans (priests); Kshatriyas (warriors); Vaisyas (merchants); and Sudras (servants). Beyond these four castes is actually a fifth, the Panchamas, the outcasts.

I was born in the south of India into the highest caste, the Brahmans. But until the defining day I am referring to, I was considered the lowest caste, a Sudra. On this day—a day that is as auspicious as auspicious can be—an initiation ceremony called the Upanayana was performed with the investiture of the sacred thread. It was only at this point that I formally became a Brahman.

Richard: Sacred thread? Why would a piece of string be considered sacred?

Subra: Hmm. This might be tougher than I thought. Let me back up for a moment. How much do you really want to know?

Richard: Well, everything, Subra. How am I ever going to understand Hinduism unless we go deeper?

Subra: Ah, wisely spoken.

You see, Richard, it's like this: every Brahman longs for a son. We believe that unless there is a son to perform the annual ceremonies in honor of our ancestors, all six previous generations will fall into infernal misery, or hell. That's what I had always been taught anyway.

So when I was born, my father was very happy. But my mother, like every Hindu woman who gives birth, was considered defiled.

On the eleventh day after my birth, a time of purification began for my mother. She was allowed to bathe for the first time since I was born, and at a formal ceremony I was given a name.

It is a very important ceremony. In it, an object is brought to the ceremony that symbolizes the boy's future. In my case, it was a silver plate holding some palm leaves. This was to suggest that my life was to be devoted to sacred studies. My mother couldn't even attend the ceremony because she was considered unclean for another thirty days.

I had been considered impure also until this eleventh day. And it was not until this ceremony that my father could hold or touch me for the first time.

Richard: You know, I'm fascinated by custom and ceremony. Sometimes I think that we in the West have lost out by having so little ceremony and custom in our culture. At the same time, these customs create a lot of questions. But that's an aside.

You didn't have a name until you were eleven days old? What

did they call you until then? And your mother wasn't even present at your naming? That seems quite chauvinistic…

Subra: Please, Richard. Let me finish before you jump to conclusions. Few things are ever as straightforward as they first appear.

According to tradition, my name was actually chosen by my aunt, my father's eldest sister. It had to include the name of a god, and the first letter needed to belong to the constellation under which I was born. The ceremony itself was performed by a priest who had the power to change my name if he felt the astrological charts indicated that he should do so.

Richard: Wow! That's quite a process.

Subra: Indeed—it's quite a ceremony. Relatives brought me gifts and sweets, and we had a big celebration.

Richard: Does every family follow that?

Subra: The devout do. Anyway, the ceremony was to commemorate my first birth. Then I had my second birth. Or actually…let me correct that. Really it was considered my first and second birth *in this incarnation*…

Richard: First and second birth *in this incarnation*? This conversation is beginning to sound a bit like a Hindu version of the American "Who's on First?" comedy routine. Hey, there's a shop up ahead. Let's stop and have a cup of coffee, Subra.

Subra: Sounds good. *[Slowing car down]* Would you like American coffee, Richard, South Indian coffee, or masala tea?

Richard: Mmm, it's hard to decide. You've spoiled me here on my visit to your country, Subra. Coffee and tea back home lack imagination unless you're willing to pay three dollars for something for-eign sounding. You know what sounds good is some chai tea—would they have that here?

Subra: Funny you should ask, Richard.

Chai tea is really only a term marketers have chosen to make tea sound fancy. *Chai* is actually the Hindi word for "tea." So saying chai tea is like saying *tea tea*.

Richard: Oh. Well, maybe we should have some *masala chai* then... I love the spicy taste. And, oh... Let's have some of that...what do you call that dessert we had awhile back? *Pukey*?

Subra: *[Laughing]* Not pukey, Richard! But close. It's called *barfi*! Remember? I can't tell you exactly why it is named as it is, but it's delicious—delicately made with milk, sugar, saffron, pistachios, and silver paper.

Richard: Sorry, I tried to remember it by making a word association. Barfi it is, but why don't they change the name? *Barfi* just doesn't sound appetizing.

Subra: You're right. But think about it, my friend. I could list all the American food that does not sound appetizing to an Indian—hot dogs, chicken fingers, hush puppies.

Richard: Okay, I get your point. Let's just keep this conversation to names and customs. So back to the second birth of your first incarnation...

Subra: Yes, the second birth of the... You know, Richard, this really is very good pukey... Ah, now you've got me saying it! Honestly! So we come to my second birth, called Upanayana, which is really the thread investiture ceremony. It is a very sacred ritual, even more so than the naming ceremony. Indeed, no Brahman can get married without this installation.

Richard: *Upanayana,* is it? An American would have a hard time even pronouncing that word.

Subra: It's not easy for a twelve-year-old Indian boy either.

You see, the night before the ceremony, total silence is in effect. The young boy has to be absolutely, totally silent. Have you ever tried to be completely silent for any length of time?

Richard: Not really. But come to think of it, total silence sounds like a good thing for some of the kids I know…

Subra: It was very hard for me. I could not utter a sound.

In the morning my parents took me to a special booth prepared for the occasion. A sacrificial fire was burning on an altar. I was completely clean-shaven—totally bald—which is never fun for a young boy. Then I was bathed. Then they gave me some sweet food to eat—I liked that part just fine—rice, clarified butter (we call it ghee), sugar, milk, and fruit.

Richard: Hmm, butter, sugar, milk—a real cholesterol booster shot.

Subra: It is considered food in its very purest form. My mother ate with me, which is an important point to note because this was the last time I would ever eat with her.

Richard: You mean she died shortly after?

Subra: No, no, no—nothing like that. In my strict orthodox upbringing, I was considered a man from this point on. As such, I would only eat with the men of the family, separate from all women, even my mother.

After we ate, the formal ceremony commenced. A teacher who conducted the ceremony called on the nine planets to be witnesses then questioned me as to my desire to become an initiate.

Once the teacher was satisfied with my answers, he entrusted me to the gods of water, herbs, sky, and earth. Then he prayed to all the gods and demons to protect me from every kind of evil. He then commanded me to walk as a Brahman from then on. That was now my new identity.

Richard: That ceremony sounds amazing! It's almost like an Indian version of a bar mitzvah, when a Jewish boy officially becomes a "son of the commandment."

Subra: Yes, it is, isn't it?

The climax of my ceremony involved a liturgical spell, or prayer, that was whispered by the priest to my father, who whispered it into my right ear. This prayer was so sacred that my right ear, into which it was breathed, was now considered sacred. And whenever I repeated that prayer, I was cleansed from sin. No woman and no low-caste person were ever to hear it. I repeated this mantra to myself every day. I was instructed to do so for the rest of my life.

Richard: So do you still?

Subra: Do I what?

Richard: Do you repeat your mantra every day?

Subra: Oh, Richard… It's a long story. Yes, I did. For quite some time anyway. But I don't anymore. But I am ahead of myself in the story. Look, we are finished with our tea. Let's get back in the car and keep driving. We are almost at Mathura, the holy city. Sometimes I think all of this is too complicated to understand…

Richard: I'm sorry. I didn't realize how emotional a subject this is to you.

Subra: It is. It has always been, Richard. Hinduism used to be my life. The memories and emotional attachments of Indian family life are very strong. It's what keeps us together. It's part of our rich heritage… *[The two fall silent for some time as the car hurtles down the road.]*

Subra: Ah…here we are at last in Mathura, Richard. Let me just pay a few rupees to this fellow to keep an eye on the car while we are gone. If we don't, I fear the hubcaps will be gone by the time we return.

Richard: Stolen hubcaps here? Even in a sacred city—the birthplace of Krishna?

Subra: Yes, and then down the road they will be sold back to us by the fellow's father. Indians are born capitalists!

Richard: Sounds to me like exploitation. That seems to happen quite a bit in any religious city. Have you ever seen all the haggling that goes on in Rome or Jerusalem?

Subra: Never been there myself. Mathura was always held out to me as the place to be. "Mathura, Mathura, fair Mathura." Mathura, the birthplace of Krishna, so it is believed.

Before Mathura was regarded as Krishna's birthplace, it was sacred to the Buddhists also. It was actually a Buddhist monastic center at one time, comprised of twenty Buddhist monasteries and about three thousand monks who resided here. But as Buddhism declined in India, Mathura became a sacred spot to the Hindus.

Richard: You don't see many traces of Buddhism here today?

Subra: Funny you should ask. Courtesy of an Afghan warlord, most all of the Buddhist and Hindu shrines were leveled sometime around

AD 1018. Within the next few centuries, the city was determined to be Krishna's birthplace, and then the Muslim Mughal Aurangzeb flattened the Hindu temple that had been built here and put up a mosque in its place.

So over the actual birthplace, there is now a mosque. A parcel of ground protruding from the barrier of the mosque is now revered as the spot of Krishna's birth. It is a situation a little similar to the mosque that exists on the site of the temple in Jerusalem—the only place the Jews have to worship is at the Western Wall of the temple.

And like Jerusalem, this has not been a place of peace. Even now, we will be searched as we enter the main temple. And by the way, there are over five thousand temples in this small city.

Richard: Human nature is the same everywhere, isn't it? Who are these women here chanting?

Subra: This is a worship center for widows. There are about two thousand widows who come here every day to chant "Hare Ram, Hare Krishna" for four hours each morning and four hours each evening. In exchange, they are given a cup of rice at noon with some lentils and two rupees, which is about five cents, and a cup of rice and lentils at dinner. If they also chant in the evening, they are paid five rupees. Four times a year they are given a change of clothes.

Richard: Sounds like quite a life. Where do these widows live?

Subra: They have a threadbare existence, Richard. But that's considered their karmic debt being paid. You know about karma, yes? It's the belief that all of one's actions in life, both good and bad, determine one's next rebirth after death. It's too much to go into in depth right now.

Richard: Yes, I've heard of karma before. Hey…what the…? Stop that!

Subra: Watch out, Richard! I warned you not to pull out your sunglasses!

Richard: Holy cow! That monkey just snatched the sunglasses right off my face. Oh, I'm sorry…maybe I shouldn't have said "holy cow."

Subra: Well, I suppose this is the right place to say those words. Here's my handkerchief—the monkey scratched you.

Richard: Any chance of getting my sunglasses back?

Subra: I doubt it. Your glasses are probably on the roof of the temple now. The monkey is looking at his reflection in the lenses. You just have to be careful here. There are monkeys by the hundreds, cows by the thousands, and, as you see, donkeys as well. They all wander freely.

Richard: Monkeys, cows, donkeys—without religion, there would be no businesses here.

Subra: *[Laughing]* You might be right about that. By the way, the tastiest barfis in the country are also made here. They are called *pedas.* It is the same basic recipe but just a little bit sweeter and richer. You can't eat too many—it's a sure mouthful on the road to diabetes. But I could think of worse ways to go!

Richard: Hmm, sounds inviting, but I think I'll pass this time.

Back to what we were talking about. How was your religious thinking shaped, Subra? You seem to know so much about Hinduism from an insider's point of view.

Subra: Richard, it's hard to tell the whole story. It cost me so much.

As you know, my family does not talk to me anymore, and it has been so painful.

When I was in college, I started to question what I had always believed. I asked simple questions at first: *Why? Who said so? Where is it written?*

But simple questions have a way of leading to much greater things. Religion is so important in our cultural experience—India is the most religious country in the world. And you don't easily question what everybody around you believes.

Richard: Religion just seems to be everywhere here.

Subra: Yes. In more ways than you might think. We commonly use many words and expressions that come from our religion, seldom asking where they originated.

For example, the word *avatar,* which means a divine manifestation, is not even used in the Gita, one of the scriptures of Hinduism. Yet the idea of avatar is fondly believed throughout India because of its implications.

An avatar is a bodily manifestation of a higher being, even the supreme being, on planet Earth. The term is primarily used for incarnations of Vishnu, the preserver god, but it's also used of highly influential teachers in other religions, including Jesus and Mohammed. Oh! I can say so much.

Richard: The Gita? I know I've heard of that before. What is it exactly, and how does it differ from the Vedas?

Subra: The Bhagavad Gita, or "Song of God," is the most sacred book of the Hindus. It's a long narrative poem, about seven hundred verses, that tells the story of a discussion between Krishna and the warrior Arjuna, who is about to fight his cousins. The flow of the Gita revolves around man's duty, which if carried out will bring nothing but sorrow. But the poem also offers hope through the way of devotion.

The Vedas, or wisdom books, are the oldest scriptures we possess—they contain everything from teachings to ceremonial instructions in detail. The Vedas are actually a collection of four books. Each book has three parts: *mantras,* hymns of praise to the gods; *Brahmanas,* a guide for practicing rituals; and the *Upanishads,* the most important part, which deals with teaching on religious truth and doctrines.

In a different category to them are the Epics—two major tales of India. The principal one is the *Mahabharata,* which contains the famed *Ramayana,* and the *Gita.* Technically, these are not considered to be on the same philosophical plane as the Vedas, but practically, they are the books most loved by Hindus. It all sounds confusing at first. The Hindu scriptures are voluminous indeed.

Here, let's sit down awhile in the shade and look at the temple.

Richard: Sounds complicated. I don't know how you ever keep all the scriptures straight. Hey, did you see that?

Subra: What?

Richard: When that cow wandered into the temple, the pilgrim over there touched it and then touched his own forehead and his heart.

Subra: That practice comes right out of the Gita. From early times, the Hindus have revered cows because of their alleged great power.

There's also a verse in the Atharva Veda that identifies the cow with the entire visible universe:

> Worship, O Cow, to thy tail-hair, and to thy hooves, and to thy form!... The Cow is Heaven, the Cow is Earth, the Cow is Vishnu, Lord of Life.[1]

Anyhow, let me continue with my story. When I started to question what I had been taught, I decided to leave home. I had no money and no place to go, so I wandered for days and weeks, finally ending up in front of a cave.

I couldn't see anything inside the cave—it was all dark and shadowy—but as I began to walk into the cave I could feel a presence there. I walked farther and farther. Some time later I was shocked to stumble upon an emaciated swami, a mystic clad in a saffron robe, sitting in silence.

The swami had taken a vow of silence and had been there a long time. There was just enough light to see that his eyes were shut. He was reflecting. Seeing him there turned my heart toward the ultimate questions as nothing else had.

Richard: How did the swami survive inside the cave?

Subra: Barely. Every now and then the villagers who lived nearby brought him meager rations.

I stayed with the swami for several weeks, and we developed a close relationship. I kept his living quarters clean and spent many hours with him just sitting and meditating.

Finally, for my sake, he wrote a few brief words, telling me that

I must leave him and that I would find the answers I was seeking elsewhere. I was devastated, but he was leaving to go on a trip himself, so I couldn't stay with him.

Weeks later I returned to the cave, still seeking spiritual illumination, and I heard a voice in the night—but it wasn't the swami's voice this time.

The voice was clear and calm, breathtaking and true. It said simply, "Follow me." I heard it, Richard. I really heard it.

I didn't know exactly where to go after that, but somehow I knew that the same voice that spoke to me there in the cave would guide me along my way.

I left the cave and met a man walking down the road who shared with me the strange and beautiful story of a babe born in a straw manger. The babe was the incarnation of the true God and had come to connect us to the true Supreme Being.

It was the first time I had ever heard the gospel of Jesus Christ. I had always been taught that there is no such thing as sin against a holy God. I always thought that acts of wrongdoing were mainly a result of ignorance and that these evils could be overcome by following the guidelines of one's caste and way of salvation.

But there on the road I saw my sin as a real act of rebellion against a perfect and holy God. And, surprisingly, I discovered who it was I was searching for—the Lamb of God who takes away the sin of the world. My life…has never been the same.

Richard: And your family?

Subra: They would have nothing to do with me after that. Neither would my community.

The voice was clear and calm,

breathtaking and true. It said

simply, "Follow me." I heard it,

Richard. I really heard it.

—SUBRAMANIAM

Richard: I'm so sorry for you.

Subra: Converting to another belief system is never easy—even when you convert to the truth. With my new faith, I had a deep and lasting joy I had never known before, but I was also troubled for my family and country—so many who had grown up believing exactly as I had believed.

I sometimes imagined what it would be like for Jesus to simply sit down with Krishna so they could hash it all out between them. Others would hear of the conversation and decide for themselves where truth lay.

It wouldn't be that far-fetched, you know. What I heard in the cave was a real voice. If Jesus has a voice, perhaps the historic Krishna has a voice also.

Perhaps if I leaned hard enough—you know, leaned into the curtain behind time—I could hear what Jesus and Krishna would say to each other.

Can you imagine that, Richard—Jesus and Krishna talking? What would each say to the other?

The image of these two great figures deep in conversation stayed with me for some time. I could not shake the picture no matter how hard I tried.

So one day I gave in. I sat down in a cow pasture and leaned in.

Richard: You "leaned in"?

Subra: As I sat in the pasture and closed my eyes, it was like a new world became visible to me. Suddenly I could see things I had never seen before.

In the distance I saw a few saffron robes hanging from a tree and two figures standing in shadows talking. It was noon, already very hot and humid for the day—one of those steamy days you encounter only in India.

As I strained to glimpse the men's faces, their identities became apparent. It was Jesus, clothed in a white robe, with sandaled feet and scars on his hands; and Krishna, the youthful prince with his ever-present flute. Can you see them, Richard, in your own mind's eye?

Let me tell you in detail about the conversation. Listen! I strained to hear what was being said...

NEW BIRTH
OR REBIRTH?

JESUS TALKS
WITH KRISHNA

Krishna: Jesus, I know you are a teacher who has come from God. No one could have performed the miraculous signs you performed if God were not with him. Is that who you truly are? A teacher from God? Who are you really, Jesus?

Jesus: I and the Father are one, Krishna. How about you, friend. Who are you, and where were you born?

Krishna: Why do you ask these questions if you already claim to know everything?

Jesus: A fair query—yet I could easily ask it of you as well. You claim to be the ultimate incarnation of all knowledge, strength, and wisdom. So why are you asking me the reasons for my questions?

Krishna: Because I sense that you are questioning my authority.

Jesus: No, I'm actually doing what I often do when someone comes to me with a question. I ask him a question in return, which prompts him to open up the conversation within his own assumptions.

Krishna: Fair enough. So let's go back to the first question—you say God is eternal, yet you were born, Jesus. Isn't there a spot in Bethlehem that supposedly marks the place of your birth? Thousands of pilgrims go there every year to celebrate the event.

Jesus: To be true, there is a spot in Bethlehem that commemorates my birth—the birth of the child. The prophets predicted long before I was born where and when I would come in the flesh. I have never denied it.

But notice that the prophet has said of me, "Unto us a child is born; unto us a Son is given…"[2]

Listen carefully to the entire prophecy, Krishna. The *child* was born, but the *Son* wasn't born. I, the Son, have existed eternally. My disciple John wrote of me: "In the beginning was the Word, and the Word was with God, and the Word was God. The Son was with God in the beginning."[3]

But how about you, Krishna? And what about this spot here, this city of Mathura? Look at the shops, the temples, the flowers, the sweets. Smell the aromas. All this is done to commemorate your coming. You were truly born here, Krishna—isn't that what is taught about you?

Krishna: I am an idea, Jesus. It doesn't really matter whether I was born or not. It is my teaching that is important. I hope the man behind the curtain heard that.

Jesus: The man behind the curtain?

Krishna: I know somebody is listening to this conversation right now, so for his sake I want to tell you clearly who I am and what I taught.

Jesus: I have an idea what you mean. But so that I hear it directly from you, why do you say *somebody is listening*?

Krishna: Because I believe all of life is a *leela*—a play, a drama. The universe is simply a cosmic puppet theater for the gods. We are simply actors on a stage. Roles and duties are all divinely assigned and beyond human control. Backstage there is always a different script. And I know there's an audience. There's always an audience at a play.

Jesus: We may disagree on the idea of a puppet show, Krishna—there is always a choice, a will, a decision. Whoever is thirsty, let him come; and whoever wishes, let him take the free gift of the water of life.[4]

But on the subject of a man listening, I would agree—when

man seeks, he finds, and when he knocks, the door is opened to him.[5] So let's continue our discussion, for I too want to talk about the nature of who you and I are and what we teach. That is why we are talking today, you and me, for the sake of the man whose ear is pinned to this curtain. His soul is struggling. He is desperate for the truth, Krishna. Let's speak of these things for his sake, not for the sake of argument between you and me.

Krishna: Agreed. There is no need for you and me to argue. You and I are complete in ourselves.

Jesus: So let's return to that very basic question: who are you, Krishna, and what do you claim? There's a reason I'm asking this question.

Krishna: Yes, I know there are actually many Krishnas in the revelation of my scriptures. But I shall not venture forth to separate them.

I, who speak to you, speak from the noble Bhagavad Gita, the sacred song and story. That is who I truly am. Some believe I am the eighth or ninth incarnation of Vishnu, one of the most widely worshiped deities in Hinduism. Vishnu is the preserver, the second god of the Hindu triad.

And you? Who are you, Jesus?

Jesus: I AM.

Krishna: That's it? Seems like a bit of a short answer, Jesus. I thought you might say that you're Immanuel—God with us—or that you're divinely born of a virgin or that you're the second member of the Trinity. Or the Savior of humankind—that you came to provide an example for living and a sacrifice for sin.

Jesus: Sometimes the shortest answer is the most complete,

Krishna. I AM. I am the Alpha and the Omega. The Beginning and the End.

Krishna: Hmm, you may have a point there, my friend. But that raises another good question. Talk to me about the *end,* Jesus. You do know that the material world is transitory—we'd probably agree on that, yes?

Jesus: Yes, I teach that man is destined to die once. But with the idea of a stage that you mentioned, let me ask you this: how do the players come onto the stage, and where do they go after they exit the stage?

Krishna: I teach that souls have existed for millions of years. They just come in different costumes. Like any man changes his clothes every day, each life is actually a death. A twenty-one-year-old man has been dying for twenty-one years in that garb.

The real life always happens backstage. To all of life there is a curtain. Reality is what happens backstage, not front stage. What happens there is merely a drama. We Indians love a good drama.

And really, that is why I am here. I came onto the stage to solve a problem between two brothers and their children. As you undoubtedly know the full story, let me just summarize the basic struggle—for the sake of the man behind the curtain!

Jesus: Please continue—for the man behind the curtain…

Krishna: The blind king Dhritarashtra had one hundred sons through his wife, Gandhari.

Jesus: You did say through the *one wife,* right?

Krishna: Yes, but it's not as overwhelming as it sounds.

Jesus: Good thing for her. Please continue with the story.

Sometimes the
shortest answer is the
most complete, Krishna.
I AM. I am the Alpha
and the Omega.
The Beginning and the End.

—JESUS

Krishna: There were two brothers, Pandu and Dhritarashtra. When Pandu, who was the king, passed away, he handed the throne to his brother Dhritarashtra. But Dhritarashtra was blind, and the kingdom was stolen by his eldest son, Duryodhana.

By the way, are these names a bit confusing to you?

Jesus: Have you ever read the book of Numbers?

Krishna: Are you questioning me again?

Jesus: No, I'm just saying that some of the names listed in the book of Numbers would turn the color of your blood. Actually, I should change that metaphor because blue blood has a whole different meaning within the context of this conversation.

Please continue your story of the brothers, Krishna.

Krishna: Blue blood. That is correct—the term *Krishna* in Sanskrit has the literal meaning of "black" or "dark" and is used as a name to describe someone with dark skin. The Brahma Samhita describes my complexion as being "tinged with the hue of blue clouds," so sometimes I'm depicted in paintings with blue or dark blue skin.

But I digress. The story continues as such: the throne actually should have gone to Pandu's oldest son.

Pandu's sons were good, honest people living in the forest. The one hundred Kaurava boys, Dhritarashtra's sons (the cousins of Pandu's sons), were raised in the court. I shall resist any extensions here, but they were really the thugs and bullies of their time. They were determined not to let the Pandu boys get the reins of the government.

Jesus: If you go to Jerusalem today, you would see a similar story being played out between blood brothers. And it gets older than that:

the notion of brother fighting against brother began right from the Garden of Eden.

Krishna: My appearance on the stage of revelation was when the one hundred Kaurava brothers went to battle with the five sons of Pandu. The war lasted twelve days, and it raised all the questions about life, war, worship, evil, good, and so on.

Subramaniam: *[From behind the curtain]* I still can't believe those one hundred brothers had one mother!

Jesus: Did you hear that, Krishna?

Krishna: Yes, I did and I have already answered that question if people like him would only read.

Our friend behind the curtain is bemused by the fact that one woman could have a hundred sons. Quite a feat, he thinks. But if he had read, he would know it is not that one woman had one hundred sons in a row.

Dhritarashtra's wife had actually miscarried one son. So a yogi came and took the fetus and, after boiling it in some herbs and nutrients, separated it into one hundred baby boys. That is exactly how it happened.

Subra: I am neither bemused nor amused. I am just trying hard to separate myth from fact.

Jesus: Separating myth from fact is what to do when you want to believe and trust in God, Subra. Stories, like stones, roll in the dust until the covering of dust and dirt is seen as the substance and the truth is swallowed up by tradition. Lean in closer, my friend. Join our conversation more fully—and you will see.

Krishna: That is the truth, you know. And the most important

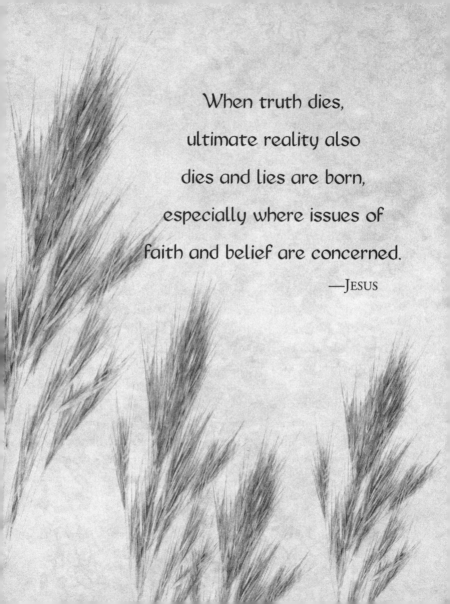

When truth dies,
ultimate reality also
dies and lies are born,
especially where issues of
faith and belief are concerned.

—JESUS

thing is the truth. Unfortunately, much is believed that is not true, and as a result, philosophies gain popularity and truth dies out.

Jesus: On that we both agree.

I was once asked, "What is truth?"[6] But the man didn't stay long enough to get an answer. When truth dies, ultimate reality also dies and lies are born, especially where issues of faith and belief are concerned.

So can I ask you then, Krishna, to explain why you have said that you are the truth and why so many have believed you? Tell me about your birth.

Krishna: It is a long story, Jesus, and I know it is really quite fantastic. When I was born—of course, no one is really born; we all pre-exist—but when I was born, it was an auspicious time. The wind blew very pleasingly. The sensation of touch was very special. Demoniac kings had been very active, and sacrifices had been interrupted.

Into this mix of some very august manifestations and demoniac threats, Vishnu appeared before Devaki, one of the demigoddesses, to intervene with her on behalf of this planet. His appearance was during the full moon. I appeared over the eastern horizon on the eighth day of the waning moon. I know there are some contradictions here—whether the moon was full or waning at first—but in the end, the moon was so overjoyed at my birth that it became full. This was because I am the Supreme Brahman, the Absolute Truth.

Jesus: Where was Brahma, the supreme deity, during this time? Hinduism teaches a three-faceted god. Where was the creator, Brahma, in all this?

Krishna: Well, that was really a tragedy.

Unfortunately, Brahma, the supreme deity, the creator, had

fallen into disfavor with the world at large because he was in love with his own daughter. Incest is strongly rejected in India, and Shiva, one of the other members of the godhead, would have none of this. So Shiva cut off one of Brahma's five heads and demoted him. Of the three in the godhead, you will notice that Vishnu is really the most popular among the people.

Jesus: Tell me about him.

Krishna: Of course. Vishnu maintains law and order in the universe. He is willing to sort of "get his hands dirty" by coming down to earth and straightening things out. He incarnates himself in different forms to come to earth and set things right.

Subra: And why is he blue?

Krishna: Vishnu is the good-looking four-armed god. He's blue because…let me just say he's blue because he's as infinite as the sky. Circling one hand is a discus that he can hurl into the air to slice up the enemies of goodness. In another hand he holds a golden baton that he uses to smash up the egos of men when they get too boastful. His third hand holds the conch shell that sounds the note of chanting. And in his fourth hand he holds a lotus, the symbol of purity.

Jesus: He existed as god before you, didn't he?

Krishna: Yes, both Vishnu and his wife, Lakshmi. It's important to mention her because she is the goddess of wealth. She's always wrapped in a beautiful red sari. She is extremely well loved because of her kindness. In fact, the masses go to her as an intercessor to Shiva, just as they come to Mary when they want to reach you.

Subra: Hang on, not everybody goes to…

Jesus: Not yet, Subra. Not yet. This conversation is far from over.

Subra: I've always been puzzled over why you leave so much unsaid, Jesus.

Jesus: Haven't you heard me warn against pouring new wine into old wineskins? New wine bursts the skin. You must first prepare the container to hold what you store in it.

Please continue, Krishna... Tell us about Shiva.

Krishna: Certainly. Shiva, he is the powerhouse, always taking care of the bad ones. You really can't miss him. He is portrayed naked because that's who he is—sheer, stark, naked reality. He is pure consciousness himself. He is covered with ashes because after the entire universe is reduced to cosmic dust, he alone will still remain. He will annihilate the universe and absorb all reality into his being.

Jesus: And he drank poison?

Krishna: As you already know, in an eternal past the gods and demons for once decided to work together to suck the nectar of immortality out of an ocean of milk. So they took a great mountain, dumped it into the ocean, wrapped the serpent Vasuki around it, and started churning. This continued for thousands of years as the gods pulled on one end and the demons on the other.

The nectar of immortality finally started to ooze out, but unfortunately, so did a poison so virulent that it started to destroy the entire world. With Vishnu's help, the purehearted gods were able to suck out the nectar. The problem was that they ingested the poison as well.

Jesus: This is where Shiva enters with his power.

Krishna: Yes, indeed. Shiva was the only one powerful enough to solve the situation. He drank the poison and held it in his throat without absorbing it into the rest of his system.

Subra: Like smoking without inhaling? I think I have heard of this in another context. And that is why...

Krishna: His throat is always stained dark...yes.

Subra: Krishna, please, these stories bring back so many memories for me. Two more stories of Shiva please.

Krishna: Which ones? There are so many!

Subra: How about the Ganesh head and the Linga?

Krishna: Hmm, why do you ask for all the questionable stories?

Subra: Questionable? I believed for years that there was sufficient truth in them to—

Krishna: Never mind what you once believed. I will tell the story for the sake of all who may be listening whom we do not see.

This is the first story. Many eons ago, Shiva's wife, Parvati (who actually goes by many different names), asked her young son, Ganesh, to guard the door to the house while she was enjoying her bath. Yes, gods and goddesses also need to bathe—that is why their statues are washed by their devotees.

While Parvati was bathing, however, Shiva returned home early from his meditation.

Actually, I need to say a little more. Shiva came home when Parvati wasn't expecting him, but he had actually been gone for so long he didn't know that Parvati had had a child, and that Ganesh was, in fact, his son. And Ganesh, of course, didn't know that Shiva was his father.

So you can imagine how upset Shiva was when Ganesh would not let him into the room where his wife was bathing. Shiva was so irritated that he took out a sickle, cut off his son Ganesh's head, and threw it away.

Jesus: I suppose his omniscience was a bit threatened here, don't you think?

Krishna: Well, gods make mistakes too, you know.

When Parvati screamed in horror, Shiva went to look for Ganesh's head but was not able to find it. So he promised Parvati he would behead the very next being who crossed his path and transplant that head onto Ganesh.

Subra: And all this while Ganesh is headless but not lifeless, I guess.

Krishna: Enough out of you, Subra!

Subra: How am I supposed to believe all this stuff if...

Krishna: *Anyway,* unfortunately for Ganesh, the next creature to come along was an elephant. Voilà, Ganesh's new head had a trunk and floppy ears—and now you know the rest of the story.

Subra: Now on to the linga.

Krishna: Yes. Well...throughout India you will see the symbol of Shiva as a linga—the phallic symbol. The male and female sexual organs are symbolic of creative power. So the linga is there to represent God's creative power and... Well, that leads to prayers for sexual prowess and fertility worship and all that.

Jesus: You know, Krishna, truth is seldom attacked head-on. It is gradually reduced until it begins to seduce a person with a mixture of half-truths and half-lies. Everything you have said so far has both a reduction and a seduction. I want us to get to that later, but first let's take a walk through this beloved city of yours.

Krishna: Yes, it is a beloved city to millions. What about our backstage friend here?

Jesus: Step closer, Subra. Step through the veil. This conversation is for you and for anyone else who wishes to hear.

Subra: I heard your voice before, saying to follow you, Jesus. That's why I was listening behind the curtain. I'm grateful to hear your discussion.

Jesus: Let's walk through the city together. Come on, Krishna. Hey, Subra—look out for that monkey!

Krishna: Oh no! Did he get it?

Subra: Ah, nuts! He got the camera case, but thank goodness I was clutching my camera. These monkeys are such a nuisance.

Krishna: Actually, they're not. Have you forgotten, Subra, that it was Hanuman, the half-monkey god, who rescued Rama's wife from the wicked clutches of the king of Lanka?

Subra: I remember that story well. Hey, be careful or you'll step on some pretty heavy cow droppings here. And watch out for these sewers. They run along this whole city and smell up—

Krishna: Don't be so critical when you are someone's guest!

Jesus: Actually, Krishna, I don't think Subra's trying to be critical. Listen to the point behind what he's saying.

On the one hand, all the ceremonies, sacrifices, and offerings are supposed to be washed and clean and pure. But look at the lives of the masses here. So many people are totally uncared for. Disease stalks every corner. The beggars outside the temple are less cared for than the cow that comes into the temple. An animal is revered and worshiped while these poor people here—made in the image of God—are ignored and scolded. What is your answer to all the darkness one finds here?

Krishna: I will also answer your question with a question. Did you not hear all the chanting that was going on as we walked by? We chant for a reason. There are about forty-eight letters or characters in the Sanskrit alphabet. *Om,* or *Aum,* is the sixth vowel with a nasal sound. When Brahma wanted to know the secret to all knowledge, the sound of Aum came to him in his mind. The more he chanted Aum, the more knowledge came to him. So really, the answer to your question can be found in chanting.

Subra: What sort of answer is that?

Jesus: Subra, please, let Krishna continue.

Krishna: Actually, the topic of chanting reminds me of another story. There is a fascinating tale about the entire epic of the Mahabharata, of which my song, the Gita, is a part.

Subra: The story of the thief's conversion?

Krishna: Yes. As you know, Valmiki was a well-known thief. He was constantly looting and deceiving people, until one day he even tried to steal from a holy man who wore only a loincloth.

But the holy man tricked the thief. He told the thief to go chant the name of the evil one, Mara, again and again, and he would get all the riches he wanted.

So the thief sat down and kept repeating, "Mara, Mara, Mara, Mara." In time it dawned on him that by chanting Mara in sequence he was actually repeating the name of Rama—the seventh avatar of Vishnu and an important manifestation of god!

See how it flows together—ma*rama*rama*rama*rama*rama*ramara. Through the chanting, the thief got his enlightenment, was changed, then penned the whole Mahabharata, all seventy-four thousand verses of it. It's considered the longest epic poem in existence.

Jesus: Human nature can be fickle and unreliable, Krishna. When I revealed myself to Moses, he wanted to know my name. In later centuries the scribes believed that God's name was so sacred they would only put markings on a page, lest they commit blasphemy by taking my name in vain. Vain chanting has no magical power, but it can have seductive power.

Krishna: We half-agree here, but I also disagree with you. Every human is created with Krishna consciousness. But due to association with time and matter, that consciousness is polluted. By chanting "Hare Krishna" and "Hare Rama" repeatedly, the transcendent consciousness within a man is awakened. The chanting produces a transcendental vibration through which all the misgivings within his heart can be cleansed away. By praising the name of Rama and Krishna, the higher energy is released and man can dance with it.

Jesus: This is where there are deep fundamental differences in our teaching, Krishna. You are using beautiful and deadly half-truths to seduce hungry hearts your way.

Krishna: Nonsense! How can something be beautiful and deadly at the same time?

Jesus: Because not everything fatal takes effect immediately. Almost all deception is initially very alluring.

Subra: May I ask a question here? Can we start with some similarities before we go to the differences between Christ and Krishna? What are the similarities in what you both teach?

Not everything fatal takes effect immediately.
Almost all deception is initially very alluring.

—Jesus

Jesus: We could talk about the similarities, but it's more important to know where we differ. I suggest we start with the false assumptions that followers of Krishna make about me. For one, that my revelation came very late in time compared to the Vedas and their writings when, in fact, long before the Vedas, Abraham was my servant and left his home in Ur to search for a city whose builder and maker is God.

Krishna: And when did Abraham do that?

Jesus: Centuries before your words were written in the Gita.

Here is another difference between what we teach. Abraham was called the "man of the tent" and the "man of the altar" in his time. This was because he understood that life is temporary and sacred. Your assertion that everyone has preexisted is totally contrary to my teaching. You teach that life, or history, is cyclical. I teach that life, or history, moves in a straight line. I teach that it is appointed to every man, woman, and child to die once and after that to face judgment before God.

Krishna: I'm so glad you brought that up, Jesus. Life is sacred, you say. Is that right?

Jesus: Yes, it is.

Krishna: Then why do your followers kill animals and eat them? Is this not the ultimate insult to life?

My devotee, Swami Prabhupada, speaks so clearly of the uncharitable West and of Christians and others who eat meat, slaughtering animals just to fill their plates!

Jesus: Let's examine that question more closely. Where would one find the best representation of your teachings—the teachings you want your followers to believe?

Krishna: In the Bhagavad Gita, my sacred song.

Jesus: And what is the context in which you did your teaching?

Krishna: What has that got to do with what I'm asking you?

Jesus: You'll understand in a moment. Please tell me the context of the Bhagavad Gita.

Krishna: Well, as you know… Pardon me, but please be patient as I answer your question. We in the East give long answers to short questions because we don't think like you Westerners.

Jesus: Bethlehem is not in the West. And more to the point, in my eyes there is no East or West, North or South. Ultimately, there is only up and down.

Krishna: I think I like you. I like the way you think, anyway. Please do not take exception to that Western slur. It is popular today and, let's be honest, Eastern words sound so much more exotic and profound. *Karma* is a much more esoteric word than *punishment* or *judgment*.

Now, about the context of my teaching… At the time, I happened to be the chariot driver of my devotee, Arjuna, who was leading the righteous Pandava brothers against the wicked Kauravas who, you remember, wanted to seize power.

Jesus: Arjuna was seeking your advice on what situation?

Krishna: Well, they were all relatives, you know. Actually, let me qualify that, because in India everybody is related. These were cousins. Arjuna was a master archer and set to lead the undermanned Pandavas against the larger army of the Kauravas. And Arjuna didn't want to have to kill his own cousins.

Jesus: Were you able to help him out of his dilemma?

Krishna: I told him that the world was a stage. This story he was involved in was just a play. The body he was afraid to kill was nothing more than a shell. Arjuna was a warrior. A warrior's duty was to kill. And he had to do his duty as a warrior in order to ensure that the kingdom would be in the right hands.

Subra: You see, Jesus, this is exactly—

Jesus: Please let me handle this, Subra. He's not fighting with you; he's trying to explain things. Please go on, Krishna.

Krishna: In the play of which we are a part, we are all born with certain duties. For the warrior, killing is his duty, the part he plays, and he should not be afraid to do it.

Jesus: This is what it all comes down to then: how can killing be a noble choice if every thing is a manifestation of the divine?

Krishna: Because as I said, the body is not important. It is just a shell. It is the soul that is important.

Jesus: So let me get this straight. In your scheme of things, it was all right for Arjuna to kill his cousins, who are part of the divine, in order for his own brothers, who are also part of the divine, to be able to rule.

Krishna: Exactly!

Jesus: But what about the lowly hamburger?

Krishna: I don't understand.

Jesus: In your scheme of things, it is not all right to kill an animal because it is a divine emblem. Correct?

Krishna: Ah…I see what you are saying. But this is a bit different. This boils down to doing one's duty, regardless of the results. What has a cow done to anyone to deserve to be killed and eaten?

Subra: Yes, the cow. Did you just see that? Have you seen the pastures here that are kept for cows and the reverence that is shown toward them, while— Look down the road and watch that man! This is so— Jesus, do you know what his principal devotee, Srila Prabhupada, the founder of Krishna Consciousness, teaches?

Krishna: He was a noble man.

Subra: When he was roundly railing against Christians for being meat eaters, and they challenged him on his teaching that the soul of an animal was the equal of the soul of a human, do you know what he said? He was asked why, if animals have souls, tigers kill and devour them. Do you know what his answer was?

Jesus: I think you'd feel better if we asked. What?

Subra: I'll quote his exact words. He said, "God is very kind. If you want to eat animals, then he'll give you full facility. God will give you the body of a tiger in your next life so that you can eat flesh very freely. Why are you maintaining slaughterhouses? I'll give you fangs and claws. Now eat. So the meat-eaters are awaiting such punishment. The animal eaters become tigers, wolves, cats, and dogs in their next life—to get more facility."[7]

That was his answer. This is utter rubbish!

Krishna: We are listening, Subra. Slow down.

Subra: Well, I guess if I want to get my say in this life, I have to fit it all in now. Who knows? According to Prabhupada, I may have claws in the next life and no ability to speak!

Don't you see what I'm getting at, Krishna? You can't have it both ways. You say that all living things have souls. Frankly, I'm not even sure what that means apart from a moral-spiritual dimension.

So you tell Arjuna that it is acceptable for him to kill his cousins because he'll only be killing their bodies. But you tell me that it is wrong to kill animals for food because they have souls and are not inferior to or different from humans.

You tell me that my punishment in the next life for my wrong-doings in this life is that I will be *demoted* to an animal. Yet, you say that animals are equal to humans and, in fact, there are gods who are half-animal and half-man.

Which is it? How can I really be expected to buy into this system? Is this really truth you are teaching, or are these just outdated fears and prejudices in the garb of religion? It is difficult to see how you can make any kind of system out of all these contradictions. I can accept that there are partial truths in Hinduism, yes, but systematic truth, no!

Jesus: The difference goes deeper than that, Subra. Much, much deeper.

Krishna: Yes, I guess there are differences between us. My reverence for the cow is just a surface issue.

Jesus: Before we leave that topic, since it is a topic of such consternation to many people, why don't you explain why you think in those terms, Krishna?

Krishna: Do you mean why do I believe in the sanctity of the cow?

Jesus: Yes.

Krishna: Prabhupada, my disciple, has explained it very clearly in his commentary on the Gita. Think about it for a moment. Raising cows fulfills the four aims of life. Through the cow, one earns wealth *(artha)*, righteousness *(dharma)*, desire *(kama)*, and salvation *(moksha)*.

Subra: I really do not want to be difficult, but am I missing something here? I'm not trying to ridicule what someone else holds to be sacred. Prabhupada's defense of the sanctity of the cow, which I have read many times, was, "Cow's milk and butter bring wealth for the nation. Cows give birth to bullocks which are used in plowing the land. The air touching the cow's body becomes pure."[8] I really don't know what he meant by that! "Her dung and urine check epidemics like plague and cholera. The urine of the cow is useful in heart diseases. Cow dung is used as manure. Clarified butter as ghee."[9] Is he serious? Is this a meaningful defense?

Krishna: Can you not see the point Prabhupada is making? He is saying that the cow sustains life for us. Without the cow, who among us would live?

Jesus: This gradually moves to the heart of our differences, Krishna. You and your followers have confused the ends with the means.

It's not the cow alone that is responsible for the milk she gives. What about the farmer who plants the grain the cow eats and milks the cow? Without the farmer, there would be no one to milk the cow. And who made the farmer? Who made the cow? Who caused the grain to grow and gave the farmer the strength to harvest the grain and milk the cow? Do you think the cow has made a conscious decision to produce milk so that you can live? Isn't it the Lord of creation who merits your worship, rather than the cow He has made?

To feed the cow, to care for it—that's all good. I have said in my Word: Do not muzzle an ox while it is treading the grain.[10] But is it about the oxen that God is primarily concerned? Surely God's concern is first for the farmer and his family before it is for the cow!

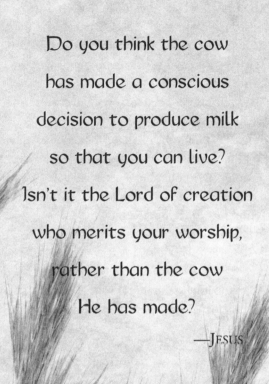

Do you think the cow
has made a conscious
decision to produce milk
so that you can live?
Isn't it the Lord of creation
who merits your worship,
rather than the cow
He has made?

—Jesus

It is God who supplies the seed to the sower. Ultimately it is God who provides bread for food. It is God who is responsible for the increase of a man's store of seed and God who enlarges the harvest. It is God who blesses the man and makes him rich in every way so that he can be generous to others, and his generosity will result in thanksgiving to God.

Krishna: I do not deny that God deserves to be thanked. But I still say that the cow is the key to life.

Subra: Without the oil that produces fuel, the teachers of what you propound would never have made it to the West to spread these teachings. Without other energy sources, we could not live. Without the laws that create boundaries for us, we would kill each other. Without procreation, the human race would be extinguished. So?

Krishna: So what?

Jesus: I get what Subra is driving at, Krishna—why do you make the means the object of your worship?

Humanity—the men, women, and children whom I have created in my image—is the centerpiece of my work. But it is God alone who is worthy of praise and worship, not the person He has created or the means He chooses to use in order to bless us. Should God worship the farmer and oil wells and sex and so on?

Subra: Where does all this stop, Krishna? You reduce yourself to nonsense! The false assertions of the revered swami about the benefits of dung and urine are the height of silliness!

I am not trying to ridicule or belittle you or what you teach. I have followed you all my life, Krishna. But I have come to the place where I don't understand why we take the blessings that come to us from God and make sacred entities out of them instead of worshiping God himself!

Jesus: This is a good point to introduce into the discussion the way that even the sacred gift of sex is used by your followers, Krishna.

Subra: I am so glad you raised this issue. Let me again quote Swami Prabhupada, who did not hesitate to make light of Christian teaching and not very subtly portray it as inferior to your way of thinking, Krishna. I have spent years thinking of these things. Here, just a minute. Let me pull out my BlackBerry and quote him directly.

Krishna: We don't grow berries here in Mathura.

Subra: No, no, I'm sorry. I'm talking about this new handheld computer, phone…whatever. Here are his exact words:

> There are many rich people in the world, but no one can claim to possess all the wealth in the world. But we know from the Srimad Bhagavatam that when Krishna was on earth he had 16,108 wives and each wife lived in a palace made of marble and bedecked with jewels. The rooms were filled with ivory and gold, and there was great opulence everywhere…nor did Krishna go to one wife one day and another wife another day. No, he was personally present in every palace at the same time. This means that he expanded himself in 16,108 forms. This is difficult for an ordinary human being but not difficult for god. He can have sixteen million and still not encounter any difficulty.[11]

This is from the founder of Krishna Consciousness. Please tell me, what I am to make of all of this.

Krishna: If you have studied and thought long on these things, you know that there are many sacred books, and it is necessary to differentiate between the stages of revelation.

Jesus: And the truth?

Krishna: Yes, of course, the truth. But as I have said, the Bhagavatam was more a leela, a play that reflected on the romantic side of my person and teaching.

Jesus: Yet, it was attributed to the pen of a man who chose the path of devotion and meditation and allegedly only wrote those words after he had reached that supreme stage of perfect knowledge.

Subra: So what do we have here? A man who has been supremely enlightened receiving revelations that are true or revelations that are bizarre?

That is the circularity of it all to me. We Hindus are given all these long treatises, and when we inquire if they are true we are simply told, "This is revelation" or "That is reflection" or "This was just a stage of understanding" or "That was added on later."

If it is possible that truth can be constantly changing, how can one possibly know what is true?

For example, Vyasadeva, who wrote the Srimad Bhagavatam, may claim these things to be just reflections in his commentary on the utmost expression of Vedic literature, the Vedanta Sutras. But the Hare Krishna followers state that this description of your 16,000-plus wives, your serenading of the milkmaids, and all the escapades about you that are related to us, Krishna, are all based on historical fact. Please tell me what am I to make of this?

Krishna: Well, you have made a good speech, Subra. May I now make mine?

Subra: Please…I am most eager for your thoughts. But before you begin, would you indulge me with one more question? I'm afraid that if I don't mention it here, I'll lose it as we proceed.

Krishna: Go ahead. I have fielded every question before and am not afraid of anything you may ask.

Subra: Some of the senseless things I hear or read from some of the holy men I have met during my travels around this country, things that are so lauded and applauded by others but seem meaningless to me, force me to ask this. My question has to do with these holy men and their supposed style of renunciation.

Krishna: What are you talking about?

Subra: Well, again, the founder of your Krishna Consciousness Movement, Swami Prabhupada, talked so much about denial to self, of freeing the mind from matter.

Krishna: Do you remember how I happened to become Arjuna's driver? He came to ask me for wisdom in waging the forthcoming battle. To his surprise, Duryodhana, the leader of the Kaurava boys, had already shown up with the same request. Because I wanted to show no partiality, I told them I would give my army to one and my presence to the other.

Jesus: That was a very profound handling of the situation.

Krishna: Yes, of course. I thought so too. I told them to go back and think about the choice I was offering them. Whoever was the first to come to me in the morning would receive his request.

Well, Duryodhana was determined to get the better of Arjuna, so he came at the first blush of dawn and sat by the head of my bed, waiting for me to wake up. I think in the West they have a very good saying: the early bird always catches the worm. But in this case, it didn't work that way.

Arjuna was in no rush. He wakened at his usual time, had his time of prayer, then came to sit at my feet.

When I awakened and sat up, naturally the first one I saw was Arjuna, sitting at the end of my bed, even though Duryodhana had come earlier. So I gave Arjuna his request first, and he asked for my presence with him. Duryodhana had my army.

Jesus: The human heart always makes the same mistake Duryodhana made—outward manifestations of might and strength.

And do you know there is a somewhat similar story in the ancient Scriptures I have revealed? When Moses was preparing to lead his people into the land I had promised to give them, he refused to go any further unless my presence would go with him.

He chose well. It is the presence of the Lord that makes the difference in the outcome.

Krishna: Right.

As I was saying, Arjuna had already been taught the multiple paths to attain release from the cycle of births.

Jesus: You're referring to the three paths for release from the prison of reincarnation?

Krishna: Yes, I am. But I think that before I continue in that train of thought, it is important that I explain my view of how life itself is shaped. Even more than a play, there are rather seasons, or *stages,* of life. Every life consists of four of these…uh…stages. We call them *asramas.*

I struggle for the right words because the words that reflect our doctrine really do not translate well into Western languages. The context is so different. To really understand and be true to my teaching, the listener needs to understand the context of the words.

Jesus: I understand what you're saying. But don't you think that can also be an escape route? Ought not the Supreme Being be able to reveal His truth to those of *every* tongue and tribe, regardless of its context?

For instance, those who follow Mohammed also make the same claim—that no one can see the miracle of the Qu'ran unless he understands Arabic.

I think we must reject such simplistic discriminations against those of a different language or group. On the day in Jerusalem when my Holy Spirit descended upon the early church, people of many different languages all heard and understood the truth as it was spoken to them. When the curtain of time is pulled down, men and women from every tongue and tribe and nation will be present with me.

Krishna: Well, let me proceed to describe those four stages of life as I see them.

The first stage is a period of discipline and education.

The second is the life of the householder and active worker.

The third is the loosening of the family bonds and attachments.

When the curtain of time
is pulled down, men and
women from every tongue
and tribe and nation will
be present with me.

—JESUS

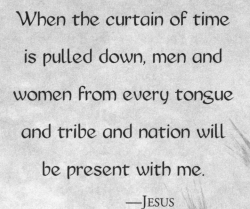

And finally there is the stage of the ascetic and the hermit.

That is why people who have not yet reached the third or fourth stage of life do not fully understand what my teachers have done when they "retire from family life." These people have fulfilled their calling at the previous stages of life and have moved toward the stage of the *sanyasin,* the stage of denial to self, of freeing the mind from matter.

When you look at them, you see only thin, weak-looking men in their saffron robes. They may look thin and weak, but they are strong in themselves. In fact, they will walk many miles every day. They have become detached from the cares of the world.

Jesus: And where does this leave the person who doesn't want to retreat from life that way, the person who wants to remain connected to the world?

Krishna: This is where the three ways that Arjuna already knew come into play. As you know, the revelation of my truth also came in stages. The Vedas culminated in the teaching of the Upanishads, and the main teaching of the Upanishads is that the essence of each individual is the *atman.* And the essence of ultimate reality is the Brahman—the impersonal absolute.

Let me illustrate. If you take a fruit from a tree and split it, you will find a seed. But if you split the seed, what do you see? Nothing! Now, just as the essence of that big tree is reduced to the impersonal nothing, so is the self reduced to nothing. The goal in life, according to the Upanishads, is to unify the self with the Brahman, the impersonal absolute.

There! Do you see it? This is to have reached the stage of denial to self, or freeing the mind from matter.

Jesus: This is very different from my teaching, Krishna. Radically different. The Supreme Being is not an impersonal absolute, but an infinite, personal Creator. God is lovingly and keenly interested in the affairs of humankind.

Krishna: Yes, you have stated that difference well. Hinduism's supreme being is impersonal, a philosophical absolute, not a personal one. That is why when people ask us who god is, we cannot give a simple answer—god is *one,* god is *all,* god is *everything.* Again, words fail us.

For this reason I revealed myself in the Gita in a very unique way. After the teaching of Gautama, the Buddha, the revelation of the divine came in a different way and showed three different ways to attain god.

Subra: To attain god?

Krishna: Yes. I am talking about more than just reaching out to god. I am talking about the possibility of *attaining* god, of actually becoming one with the divine. The paths to moksha, or freedom from reincarnation, are said to be many.

Let me explain it a bit more. Salvation in Hinduism is attained in one of three general ways with slight variations. The first is the way of knowledge. It is called *jnana,* which as I'm sure you both know, is the word for wisdom or knowledge.

The second is the way of *karma,* the path of works.

And the third is the way of *bhakti,* the way of devotion and love.

Subra: Defining God and salvation may be complex, but I must challenge the simple way in which you are explaining it. You are saying that while God is not personal, you can claim to be God. And *you* are certainly personal—you are supposed to be an avatar, one of the incarnations of God.

Buddha was also supposed to be an incarnation of God. Yet Buddha denied a supreme being. There is not one mention of God in Buddhism.

Krishna: Have I even used the word *avatar* in my Gita?

Subra: No, you haven't. But you have already acknowledged that you are an incarnation of god. And you mention the preexistence of every soul and the reincarnation of every life.

Krishna: Yes, but perhaps I could finish what I was saying. It is very important that you hear what I said in the Gita. We both know that the Vedas teach that god is an ultimate impersonal absolute.

Subra: So do you dispute that?

Krishna: I find no need to dispute it. I just *transcend* it. I represent god as a very personal being.

Subra: What about the others— Shiva, Vishnu, and Brahma?

Krishna: I am them. I am Vishnu. I am Shiva. I am the heavenly father. I have spun this universe. I am the ruler. I am the supreme god.

Subra: You are God incarnate and have come before?

Krishna: All that was seen in Vishnu and Shiva and Brahma is in me. All the devotion of the human heart must be directed to me. I am all the heart yearns for.

Jesus: I wonder, Krishna, if you are the divine one, are the sacrifices demanded in the Vedas offered to you?

Krishna: Yes, of course. Various canons of our scripture have given specifics for sacrifices. But these sacrifices are only shadows. I told Arjuna that such sacrifices only led to more sorrow and rebirths. The true sacrifice is god himself.[12] So I am both the one to whom the sacrifice was made and the sacrifice itself.

Subra: The true sacrifice is God Himself! That is a most startling assertion. That's what I was waiting to hear!

Jesus: Wait, Subra. Wait a little longer. More needs to be said yet.

Krishna, who is this god you are describing, the god who has sacrificed himself? Is this the attribute-less god of the monists, or does this god have the attributes of the dualists?

Krishna: God is the same. God is both the one to whom no attributes may be assigned and the one of whom attributes may be assigned. It is the same. I have come to transcend all of the revelations.

Jesus: So if all devotion is to be given to you, how does someone come to you?

Krishna: You know, that is the question Arjuna asked me also.

Jesus: I'm aware that he did and that he isn't the only one who has asked this question. It is the question of every aching and every honest heart: *how do I approach God?*

Krishna: I believe this is a very difficult question to answer in the light of the preceding revelations.

Jesus: It may be difficult, but it is not impossible.

Krishna: Let me go back to the questions of Arjuna as he faced his cousins.

I told Arjuna that if he forgot his own duty and honor and did not take part in this righteous war, he would be sinning.[13] I explained to him the crux of karma yoga: "The work alone thou hast right, but never the fruits thereof. Be thou neither actuated by the fruits of the action, nor be thou attached to inaction. O Dhanajaya, abandoning attachment and regarding success and failure alike, be steadfast in yoga and perform thy duties."[14]

Jesus: What did you say to him about the other ways to approach God?

Krishna: That the way of knowledge is also profitable. I told him that just as fire reduces all action to ashes, the attainment of wisdom purifies the effort to think not of its results but of its moral obligation. I think it is impossible to explain so that you can truly understand what a difficult task it was for me to transcend teaching without undermining it.

Subra: Indeed it is, but I think that part of the problem is that nothing in Hinduism is ever really annulled. It is either dealt with by silence or just purposefully ignored. For example, what about the caste hierarchy?

Krishna: I did not annul it, but I maintained that a person of any caste can attain moksha, or salvation.

Jesus: Ah yes, but you also added that the reason they were part of the lowest caste was because their previous life of sin had caused them to descend the scale of the caste system.

Krishna: That is correct. I did not deny that punishment of one life follows into the next.

Jesus: But there is also an attainment that eradicates differences in a dramatic fashion.

Krishna: Yes, one who has attained the utmost liberation sees no difference between a Brahman, a cow, a dog, or an elephant. All are the same level of being.

Subra: This is what is so puzzling to me—the very thought that animal life is a demotion to start with but an enlightened mind sees no difference between an animal and a person.

Jesus: We'll get to that, Subra. Be patient. We're making real progress in our conversation. Truth is powerful. And truths that are almost truths are deadly and seductive. We'll see the difference.

Where in all of this then, Krishna, is the means of attainment? You have dealt much with the types of yoga for liberation—please spell them out here once again.

Krishna: The types of yoga for liberation... As I know you are already aware, Patanjali systematized yoga into eight stages. The final stage of yoga is union with the absolute and the annihilation of mind. The *advaitin* or nondualist, also taught the cancellation of the mind. Buddha, in fact, talked of the realization of the cancellation of self. That is why I focus on karma yoga, which is not physical exercise, but nurturing the spirit of self-denial and desirelessness of deed in utter devotion to god. *Bhakti,* love and *sharanagati,* surrender, are two key words. Love and surrender are the easiest of all the disciplines.

Now, all of these paths of knowledge and works are good, but there is a supreme path. And that is the path of devotion. I wish for them to live in the beauty of my love.

Jesus: There was a man who once came to me and asked, "What must I do to attain eternal life?"[15] He was sincere. I told him to keep the commandments.

Krishna: What did he say?

Jesus: Well, my answer was actually intended to give him something other than what he intended to receive.

Subra: Your first response to him was what captured me. You remember, when he called you "good"?

Jesus: Subra, you are an irrepressible man. You really want to say so much, don't you?

Subra: I'm sorry! It's just that…

Krishna: Can I hear what this is all about please?

Jesus: When the man came to me he called me "Good Master," and I questioned his salutation. "Why do you call me good?" I asked. "There is none good but God."

Krishna: Well, I think that is not exactly right. There are a lot of good people in the world.

Jesus: I questioned his notion of goodness so that he would have to concede that by calling me good, he was really calling me "God." Otherwise he would have had to assert that there is goodness apart from God. That is at the heart of the meaning of salvation and how we come to it.

Krishna: I'm listening. Why did you stop?

Jesus: Because we must weigh each assertion at the starting point of every belief. What I said made him uneasy, so I told him what he wanted to hear. I said, "Just go and keep all the commandments." He surprised himself, I think, by answering that as far as he knew, he had kept all of them. Then I told him to go and sell all that he had and give the money to the poor and then follow me.

Krishna: That sounds so much like what Buddha would have said.

Jesus: No, Buddha would have said, "Sell all that you have and give it to the poor. *And then follow the path.*"

Krishna: You are right—I see the distinction.

Jesus: These kinds of mistakes, Krishna, are at the heart of the substantive difference between us. Just because two things have one thing in common doesn't mean they have everything in common. The heart of humanity and the provision of God are the two central points we must understand.

Krishna: I am not so sure of what you call the substantive differences between us, Jesus. For instance, you yourself teach reincarnation.

Jesus: Where did you get that from?

Subra: If I may intervene, I'm sure he's referring to the time your disciples asked you whether the man you all met who was born blind was born that way because of his own sin or because of his parents' sin.[16]

Krishna: Thank you. That's right.

Jesus: All right. And what did I answer him, Subra?

Subra: You said it was neither.

Jesus: Well?

Krishna: Well, what? I do not understand your answer! You talk in riddles!

Jesus: My disciples were making an assumption when they asked their question—that the man's blindness was the result of sin, his own

The heart of humanity
and the provision of God
are the two central points
we must understand.

—JESUS

or his parents'. My answer dispelled their assumption. There was no connection between sins and his blindness.

Subra: You bring up an interesting point, Jesus. I was reading the other day that two-thirds of the people with leprosy in the world are in India. And more than half of the people with blindness in the world are in India. Karmic logic would lead me to the conclusion, then, that India has sinned more than the rest of the world. This is such pathetic reasoning that I don't know whether to be angry or sad!

Jesus: You're getting the point, Subra. It's neither particular nor personal sins that bring tragedy into the human situation; it's the state of sin humanity is in that has broken its relationship with God. Alienation from God has resulted in a suffering world. This must be understood.

Subra: We do have more than our share of poverty in India. Look around. There are so many sick, so many people with deformities. Yet in a strange way, the human spirit is still unsuppressed all throughout India. To India's credit, it still seeks after the Supreme. People here still long for the touch of love and to belong. We don't hold our condition against God.

Jesus: But you hold it against yourselves, and that's the tragedy of reincarnation.

Krishna: So you do not teach the sacred doctrine of reincarnation?

Jesus: No, I do not. As I said before, it is appointed to every person to die once, and after that comes judgment.[17] Reincarnation, or repeated births, makes no sense when a person has no idea what the previous births were and what decisions he or she made that resulted in their present life. They don't know what they are paying for, or how to pay for it, or when they have paid it.

Subra: But all the great religions of the East teach the doctrine of rebirth, don't they? And Christianity is a religion of the East.

Jesus: Subra, you've bought into too much Western thinking with that question.

First, I don't like the designation "of the East." True, I entered a very Eastern setting when I came into the world. But don't make the mistake of restricting God geographically or linguistically.

The insistence of the followers of Mohammed that the miracle of his revelation is in one particular language and that it can only be recognized if you understand that language is an absurd claim!

The Vedic sages seized for themselves the authority of interpretation—that only they can interpret truth. That is also absurd.

I say that even a little child can come to me and understand the truth I bring. I am not the private possession of one people or one language or of one level of education or understanding. I came into the world for *all* of humankind, regardless of who they are, what language they speak, or where they live.

Krishna: But Subra is still right, you know. All religions of the East *do* teach that every birth is a rebirth.

Jesus: I don't teach that, nor do Muslims believe it.

Krishna: That is true, I guess. But Gautama, the Buddha, did.

Jesus: Not quite. He didn't believe there was such a thing as a *self.* So rebirth to him was a karmic rebirth, not an individual rebirth.

Buddha did not believe that an individual was reborn, only that their good or evil deeds had to be atoned for by someone else. He rejected your call to devotion to the Supreme. There is really a world of difference between his teaching and yours. That's why Buddha turned his back on Hinduism.

Krishna: If every birth is not a rebirth and karma is not carried over into the next life, what is your teaching on restitution and individual responsibility?

Subra: Before you answer that, Jesus, I would like to ask Krishna another question on rebirth if I may.

Krishna: Why am I not surprised?

Subra: If I am now in the long sequence of rebirths, and in every birth I am paying the dues from my previous birth, can you tell me what I was paying for in my first birth? And please don't say that there are an infinite number of preceding births, because if there were, I never would have reached this one!

Jesus, why are you smiling right now?

Jesus: It's a difficult question that you've just posed to Krishna. It's a question for which you'll be accused of being "too interested" in knowing what happens behind the curtain. Yet the very rejection of the legitimacy of your question is based on having the right to look behind the curtain. So I too await the answer.

Krishna: Humph! Some things will always be hidden from view because the mind cannot understand them.

Subra: It figures! Krishna, I must completely reject that answer because it is an escape. I'm not trying to probe a mystery. I am trying to understand the heart of reincarnation as you teach it.

Jesus: The problem, Krishna, goes deeper than Subra's question. You asked me what I would say about restitution and individual responsibility. Let's frame the question this way...

Come with me on an imaginary journey to Calcutta. Let's walk for a moment into the Kali Temple. Mind the people along the way as you walk. These are the masses, who hunger both physically and spiritually. Don't blame their condition on karma.

Subra: Jesus, isn't this the city to which the missionary William Carey came with the gospel in the late 1700s?

Jesus: It is, and it was through him and some notable Indian reformers that certain terrible practices of those times were stopped—among them the forced suicides of millions of widows.

The plight of the widow has always been difficult for an unindustrialized, agrarian society. How is she supposed to earn a living now that her husband has died? So many Indian widows once leaped into the flames of the funeral pyres on which their dead husbands were laid or were tied to their husbands' pyres so they wouldn't be a burden on their families. These practices were ended by the efforts of Carey and others who saw the injustice of it all.

Krishna: Why are you wanting to bring all this up? What has this to do with our conversation?

Jesus: Because belief is a contagious thing, often carried by the force of culture, and the truth behind a belief is often missed. My own people once came to the point of offering their children as sacrifices, thinking they were doing God a service.

But let's go back to the Kali Temple today. Come over here to the altar, and watch what happens.

Subra: This is very discomforting.

Jesus: Do you see the priest over there, with his huge knife? Do you see that family, dragging the little black goat by a rope?

Subra: I have seen this thing before.

Krishna: I know what this is all about. What is the point of bringing us here?

Jesus: Do you see the goat's head being placed in that hollowed-out place on the altar? Watch the blade come down. See the goat's body quiver. See the priest fling away the carcass. Now watch. Watch the penitents, the family members, put their fingers in the fresh blood and mark first their foreheads and then their white clothes with it. Now Subra, go over there and ask the priest why the penitents have marked themselves that way.

Subra: Is it really necessary that I do that? That priest doesn't look as if he will be very happy to entertain my question.

Jesus: Please do as I ask you, Subra.

Subra: *[Returns]* Did you see how he reacted to my question?

Krishna: Of course, he is upset! What did you expect? You are intruding upon his sacred duties!

Subra: But in the name of reason, why can't one ask a question? Why can't one try to understand what is happening and what it means?

Krishna: You cannot just question centuries of belief and ritual!

Subra: That simply is not right! If I am to believe it, I must know what it means! But anyhow, he just brushed me aside and said, "Nothing!"

Krishna: *Nothing* what?

Subra: I asked him what it all meant and why they marked their foreheads and clothes with the blood. He said, "Nothing!"

Jesus: This is the tragedy of ceremony and ritual. This was the most solemn thing this family could do in their efforts to reach God. Yet the priest himself said it all meant nothing.

Krishna: I am certain that he did not literally suggest that it means nothing. He was just offended that you were intruding upon a practice that had nothing to do with you.

Jesus: No, Krishna, no. This is exactly what I warned against. I told my people to put markers in the city and on the memory block of time so that when their children asked why something was done or what something meant, they would be able to answer that it was done to the glory of God and to remind them of all God had done for them. But priests and teachers so often bring money and corruption into religious practice, assuming a position before people and refusing to be accountable for what they believe and how they live.

Subra: This has been my biggest complaint against so much organized religion.

Jesus: Yes, they build big buildings to display their talents and power. They demand money from people. Instead of teaching the truth, they tickle the ears of their listeners and prey upon innocent and unthinking minds. Oh, the power of religious leaders! All their vain chantings and speeches, and when one asks what it all means, they do not even bother to try to give an explanation!

The life of a little goat was taken here. Goats give milk too, you

Instead of teaching the truth,
they tickle the ears of
their listeners and prey
upon innocent and unthinking
minds. Oh, the power of
religious leaders! All their
vain chantings and speeches,
and when one asks what it
all means, they do not
even bother to try to
give an explanation!

—JESUS

know, Krishna. They sustain life in the same way that cows do. But the goat was slaughtered before your eyes, and when you ask what it means, the priest says, "Nothing!"

Subra: What *does* it all mean? I really do not understand it. Why this shedding of blood? Why all this mess in the temple?

Jesus: This is where my teaching is so different from any of these religions. Oh, Krishna, of all teachers you came the closest to what I taught. You were the most similar to me in the solution you brought to the problem of the human heart. But you stopped short! Your exhortations to Arjuna were profound. But it is not only what you said that fell short of the answer; what you did NOT say and what you could NOT do also fell short of the truth.

Krishna: Well, at least we have some common ground.

Jesus: Yes, we do, but it is the uncommon ground that is important. It is on the uncommon ground that you meet the One who created life and breath and who offers salvation, forgiveness, and restitution.

Subra: I have been waiting to hear the main difference. Please tell me.

Jesus: First and foremost, every person's place of birth is sacred in the sense that I have purposefully created every man, woman, and child. I determined from the beginning where each one was to be born. The race of each and every person is sacred. No race is superior to another.

And I am not far from any one of them. Great followers of mine have come from this very nation—people like Sadhu Sunder Singh, Bakht Singh, and Pandita Ramabai. They were born in this great land. They called upon me, and I answered them.

But they learned that you cannot be righteous until you are first redeemed. It is not rebirth that they learned from me, but a *new* birth that is made possible by my Holy Spirit.

Subra: That alone challenges the caste system, doesn't it?

Jesus: Every religion, it doesn't matter which one you name, creates a system of approaching God or some formula to find bliss and ultimate purpose.

Most, if not all, give you a path to follow, a way that helps you do certain things—observe certain laws, pay certain monies, establish certain hierarchies, erect certain buildings, ordain certain priests, and select places or directions of prayer. And only then can you come to the purpose God has for you.

Subra: Yes, that is true. I have seen it and read it for myself. I have memorized pages of demands and directions so I would not forget all that was expected of me. I believe religion is a way of controlling people, and that it is often a guise for political power.

Krishna: Can I say something here? I would like to say that in many ways, the advantage of my teaching is that it adapts itself to the person who is seeking. I have said so many things in so many different ways so that each person is able to interpret it for himself and determine his own level of understanding and teaching.

Jesus: Are you saying that there is no absolute way?

Krishna: Yes! That is correct! But there is still an absolute destiny. Some may come the way of knowledge. There are very few who have that capacity.

Others find the way of works and service. I say to them this: possessing a pure intellect; with senses fully under control; casting aside attraction and aversion; living in solitude; eating little; controlling speech, body, and mind; always engaged in meditation and concentration; having no passion; having given up egoism, force, arrogance, desire, anger, and accumulation; devoid of the notion of "mineness"; and being peaceful; such a man is qualified to attain Brahma, the absolute.[18]

Subra: I simply cannot accept that possibility. That is total renunciation. I mean, it is an escape from reality. And it is impossible to achieve.

Krishna: But it is precisely what I am calling for. He whose intellect is unattached everywhere, who has no thirst for enjoyment, and who has controlled his mind reaches the state of actionlessness.[19]

Jesus: All those methods ignore some of the most fundamental realities of life—no one is justified by keeping the law. No one. Not one person has ever attained perfection by keeping the law. And what's more, no ritual in and of itself can bring you to God—there is no political or social cause whereby the heart is made absolutely pure.

In fact, the priests and teachers are the most accountable to me because instead of setting themselves above everyone else, their calling is to show that every man and woman is a priest before me. You do not need a priest to come to me. You can come to me directly. The teachers and ministers and sages are not superior to the simple child who comes to me with an open heart. The office of spiritual shepherd is given for a purpose—to lead others to me—but never to become the means of coming to me.

Subra: What about all these sacrifices in the Hindu temple? What good are they then?

Jesus: You heard Krishna say something fascinating a little while ago. He said that *he* was the sacrifice.

Subra: Yes, I did hear him say that.

Jesus: In what way were you the sacrifice, Krishna?

Krishna: I am the sum total of religion and devotion to which the human heart aspires.

Jesus: But what do you mean when you say that *you* were the sacrifice?

Krishna: From the beginning of Vedic ritual, sacrifices were offered as a means to come into the presence of the divine. Vedic teaching is rich in this, and the priests were given all the instructions on how to conduct the sacrifices. I was pointing out to you that I was the ultimate expression of it all.

Jesus: That is what I meant when I said that you came the closest to the truth but stopped short. How are you the sacrifice? Yes, there is a path. Yes, there are means. Yes, there is a barrier between God and humanity.

But the heart is not separated from God because it is unethical or immoral. No amount of moral rectitude can bridge the separation between God and humanity, between God and each human heart.

I paid the price to reconcile God to man and change the human heart by the power of God.

Subra: This is the hardest thing to explain, Jesus, and in fact, the hardest thing to understand.

Jesus: I know it is. But implicit in this is the greatest truth of all—

that no one becomes closer to God by doing good works. In fact, because of the pride of the human heart and pride in one's culture, depending upon one's good works to bring one to God often becomes the biggest snare of all.

The "good" person assumes they have a hold on truth. Cultures assume they are superior to others. The pride within the human heart is the cancer of the soul.

No one, no culture, has a hold on truth. No heart escapes the stranglehold of pride. It is what brought Lucifer to his fall. The person who in his own eyes thinks he has kept the law to the fullest and by his own strength is actually furthest from God.

You see, no one can truly come to God without a sense of spiritual poverty within himself. Only when a person recognizes that all his goodness and accomplishments amount to nothing before God will he then seek God. Only in this humility can a person accept the new birth I give. The new birth gives new hunger—hunger for righteousness. As the man is now born of God by the power of God, he begins a new life for the glory of God.

Subra: Is this the heart of the difference?

Jesus: This is the beginning of the difference. You see, a man can recognize his spiritual poverty, renounce the world, don sacred attire, punish himself with deprivation, walk miles, relinquish all material belongings or ties to this world, and feel he has established his own means to attain perfection or to find God.

This is where the sacrifice comes in. Krishna said that he was the sacrifice but couldn't describe how that description fits him. Do you remember what the Scriptures say about this, Subra?

Subra: About the way you provided for us?

Jesus: Yes. I came into the world not to live—because I have always existed. I came into the world to die, not as an example to others and not to pay a penalty for myself. I came into the world to die—to show the horror of sin that separates the human heart from God's heart.

Subra: Yes, for many years I meditated on the great distance, the absolute distance, between where my heart was and where it needed to be. I often wondered how I could ever reach the heart of God.

Jesus: This is so foreign to cultures that have bought into the lie of materialism—that *matter* is all that matters. These cultures simply can't understand the nature of spiritual reality and of being separated from God. Professing themselves to be wise, they have become fools. No one today can talk of sin and be taken seriously by the cultural elites. They will call sin anything but what it is and will not accept the truth because even in their wretchedness they wish to be autonomous.

Subra: That is why I had to reject the notion that there is no absolute way. Some ways simply must be wrong. Which means that there *must* be a way that is right!

Krishna: To be sure, there are wrong ways, but the serious seeker finds that out by intuition.

Jesus: If one could discover the truth by intuition, why was there a need for revelation? If one could find the truth by intuition, why was there need for a sacrifice? If one could find the truth by intuition, why was there a need for instruction?

Krishna: Because it is all part of the drama. True religion in anyone

If one could discover the
truth by intuition, why was
there a need for revelation?

—JESUS

comes from sincerely following the path, and at the end, ultimate reality is made known to him or to her.

Jesus: Here again, Subra, we come to another core difference. I did not come to offer a religion. I did not come to offer a system of rules by which a person reaches the right destination. I am not so much interested in pointing you to a place as I am in pointing you to a Person and a relationship. That is the key.

You have heard Krishna talk about the paths, the disciplines, the stages, the levels of attainment. But I tell you that anyone can come into my presence because I am the way. I have come so that you can have the indwelling presence of my Holy Spirit.

Subra: I went through so much looking for the way into God's presence. I did not understand how simply profound and profoundly simple it was.

Krishna: If all of this is not a drama that we are part of, being played out on the stage of history, can you tell me how you are able to stand by and watch as men, women, and children have died and continue to die—your people, the Jews—even though they follow the Old Testament, the very Scriptures you gave?

Jesus: You have asked a very deep and, yes, a very disturbing question.

When I revealed myself to the children of Abraham and Isaac, I made a covenant with them. They were to honor me with their lips and hearts to show the world what the commandments of God looked like when they were lived out.

I revealed myself in dramatic fashion. In the times of Moses, Elijah, and John the Baptist and in my own incarnation in particular, I showed myself to the Jews through many miracles—their deliverance from slavery in Egypt, their battles with so many enemies, the miracles I performed on their behalf.

When I revealed myself so dramatically to them, acknowledged by their own priests and by the people themselves, the judgment upon them had to be equally dramatic when they forgot who I am and turned their backs on me. To whom much is given, much shall be required.[20]

Responsibility is always proportionate to revelation. When people acknowledge a miracle, why are they surprised at the judgment that follows when grace is disregarded?

Subra: I had another question too, Jesus. It's really an observation. *Krishna* sounds so much like the consonants of *Christ*. Brahma sounds much like Abraham, the patriarch of the Jews, Muslims, and Christians…

Jesus: Yes, some similarities exist. Jupiter was worshiped by the Romans, Zeus Pater by the Greeks, Dyaus Pitar by the Babylonians. All those names are transliterations of the same word.

Subra: Come to think of it, Jesus, *daya* and *pita* in the Hindi language actually mean "mercy" or "pity" and "father." Is it possible that the Merciful Father is implicit in some form in all of this?

Jesus: I have not left myself without witness before any people group, Subra. I have spoken in different manners and at different times. In the past I spoke through prophets until it was time for me to come myself to this earth. Still, it is important to think not only of the similarities but also of the differences.

Krishna: But that is where you end up dividing everyone.

Jesus: Truth will always divide, Krishna. In making the very statement you just did, you are dividing truth from falsehood. A single, minute difference in the ecology of the world and you will end up with death. Miscalculation is the reason for death. Those who change my laws miscalculate the nature of the human heart. If you believe one lie, you are often led down the path of many lies.

Krishna: All right, then. If you are the sacrifice and your death provided restoration between God and man, why are people still dying? Even your own followers still die!

Jesus: That's the difference between a drama and reality. Reality cannot by wiped out by a whim. Look at that truck, trying to make its way over the pavement and the road.

Subra: In America I think they would call it the shoulder…

Jesus: Yes, they would. But right now I'm in the East, speaking to one from the East. They'll make their own translation.

Look at that truck, Subra, and at its shadow on the sidewalk. Now tell me this; would you rather be run over by the truck or by its shadow?

Subra: By the shadow, of course. That is not difficult to decide.

Jesus: Is the shadow real or imaginary?

Subra: It is real.

Jesus: Yes, it is, because the truck momentarily blocks out the sun, which creates the shadow. You don't judge by the shadow; you judge by the light.

That's the story of the gospel. When I died on the cross for you and for every person born onto this earth, the truck of the judgment and penalty of the law went over me so that only the shadow of death would pass over you. You still have to face the pain of death, but I have paid its price. It was I who was crucified, but my disciples are still troubled and heartbroken by the shadow of death.

Subra: How can one not be heartbroken when one sees the heartbreak of the world?

Jesus: Yes, I wept by the grave of my friend Lazarus too, Subra. I wept even though I knew I was going to raise him from the dead. I will never ignore what is real. But I will be with you through all pain, even death.

When I rose again from the dead, the disciples were so certain of who I was and of the truth I had brought them that they were willing to pay the ultimate price to take this truth around the world—because they loved me and knew I loved them and the world. For the sake of the gospel—the payment for sin and provision for the restitution of every person before God that I accomplished in my death—they endured suffering, as I had. The Son shone in His power over death and sin and the grave.

Krishna: This concept of shadow and reality is fascinating.

Subra: It is just like Plato's shadow.

Jesus: Not quite. In the shadows of Platonic thought, they saw goodness but never God. And many followers of religion make the same mistake. They see shadows of good and evil, but they never see God. The difference may seem tiny, but the implications are great.

Krishna: Why do you always focus on the differences?

Many followers of religion
make the same mistake.
They see shadows of
good and evil, but they
never see God.

—JESUS

Jesus: I think you're missing the point, Krishna. You have a caste system and reincarnation, which focuses on the differences between people.

I came to show that there is no difference in the human condition. Every one—East, West, North, or South; rich or poor; educated or not—falls short of the glory of God. In every person's own efforts to reach God, he falls short.

The difference I am talking about is how each of us responds to the shadow reality or the concrete reality. You say there is no difference between an animal and a human being, but at the same time you say that an animal is in that form because he is a human being who's being punished for a previous life. While the difference between the DNA of the two may be minute, the implications for language, reason, and worship are defining.

I commanded my people to treat the animal with respect because it too is my creation. But humans alone were given the supreme privilege of worship and of a relationship with the God who made them. A human's decision to reject me or trust in me is an eternal difference.

Krishna: I can certainly see that the differences are critical.

Jesus: They are, Krishna. So I ask you again not just why you spoke of sacrifice yet never offered it but, I ask you, did you ever really live?

Krishna: To me it does not matter.

Subra: You know, Jesus, some of the greatest scholars say that Krishna was an imaginary figure, or else they downplay the historicity of his person because of the many Krishnas in Hindu writings...scholars like

Radhakrishnan, Vinoba Bhave, Aurobindo Ghosh, Vivekananda, and Mahatma Gandhi.

Jesus: That is the hatpin to the heart of reality. To many the shadow, or the idea, is good enough. But for me and for those who follow the truth, the facts and acts of history are critical. It's not land or power or cities or control over governments that matters. That I was born, lived, died, and rose again from the grave are real acts of history. My Scriptures are historical documents in which geography and history can be the testing points of my claims. Jerusalem, Bethlehem, Calvary, and the empty tomb are actual places. And just as concrete and real is the new birth and the communion with me that I offer to all who ask.

Subra: That is the difference between you and Jesus, Krishna. It is why I have become a follower of Jesus. At best, you were a shadow. But in Jesus I found the real thing.

Krishna? Krishna? Where did you go?

Jesus: I think you know the answer, Subra. Krishna has left the theater because the play is over. When you deny reality completely, there can be no actors left.

The shadow seeks to block the sun. But I am the light. I am the Son. In me there is no darkness at all; the shadow has been dispelled. And in their efforts to please a shadow god or the gods of their own imagination, men will continue to sacrifice their sons and daughters until they receive the Son whom my Father has already provided. I came to give life; therefore, choose it.

—•—

Subra: Richard, this is the day I am waiting for—the day when all the shadows are removed and the light stands supreme. I remember the words to a hymn I heard in church:

Hold Thou Thy cross before my closing eyes;
Shine through the gloom and point me to the skies,
Heaven's morning breaks, and earth's vain shadows flee;
In life, in death, O Lord abide with me.[21]

Richard: That's beautiful, Subra. Jesus doesn't take off backstage and leave you. He abides.

I have a question. If all the world is a stage, who is the audience? Is every audience also on stage, and we see endless audiences on endless stages, each thinking they are the actors when they are really the audience... I don't know.

Subra: Were you listening, Richard? When you see a movie through a projector, the beams of light carry the picture, but you cannot see the picture without a screen to receive the projection.

I believe that I have seen both the beams and the picture. The beams carry the particles, the bits and pieces that make up the whole; the screen reveals the picture.

Richard: I guess it's time to find our car and get back to the divided highway that is not really divided...and risk death. I guess there's a metaphor there, too, isn't there? When you don't make a distinction between truth and fiction?

Subra: For the Hebrews, Richard, I have learned that the ultimate was expressed in the metaphor of light. The metaphor the Greeks used was knowledge. And for the Romans, it was glory.

That is why the apostle Paul, a Hebrew who studied in a Greek city and was a citizen of Rome, expressed it to the Corinthian church this way, "God who caused the light to shine out of darkness has caused His light to shine in our hearts to give to us the light of the knowledge of the glory of God in the face of Christ Jesus our Lord."[22]

I wonder how he might have said it had there been Indians in the audience?

Richard: Any ideas?

Jesus: He would have added one line: "That is the story to tell to the nations."

A discussion guide on the topics covered in *New Birth or Rebirth?*
is available free of charge at www.waterbrookpress.com.

NOTES

1. Atharva Veda X:10.
2. Isaiah 9:6.
3. John 1:1–2.
4. Revelation 22:17.
5. Matthew 7:7.
6. John 18:38.
7. A. C. Bhaktivedanta Swami Prabhupada, *The Science of Self-Realization* (Los Angeles: Bhaktivedanta Book Trust, 2003), 87. Available online at http://www.krishnamedia.org/e-books/Science_of_Self-Realization.pdf.
8. "Land is purified by (the following) five (modes, viz.) by sweeping, by smearing (it with cowdung), by sprinkling (it with cow's urine or milk), by scraping, and by cows staying (on it during a day and night)." *The Laws of Manu,* chapter 5, number 124.
9. *The Laws of Manu,* chapter 5, number 124.
10. 1 Timothy 5:18.
11. A. C. Bhaktivedanta Swami Prabhupada, "Krishna Is All-Attractive" (lecture, Los Angeles, 18 May 1972).

http://www.prabhupadaconnect.com/lecture_2.html (accessed 6 November 2007).

12. Bhagavad Gita 8:4; 9:16. See also Bhagavad Gita 3:14; 4:32.
13. Bhagavad Gita 11:13.
14. Bhagavad Gita 11:13.
15. Mark 10:17–23.
16. John 9:1–41.
17. Hebrews 9:27.
18. Bhagavad Gita 18:51–53.
19. Bhagavad Gita 18:50.
20. Luke 12:48.
21. Henry F. Lyte, "Abide with Me," 1847, public domain.
22. 2 Corinthians 4:6.

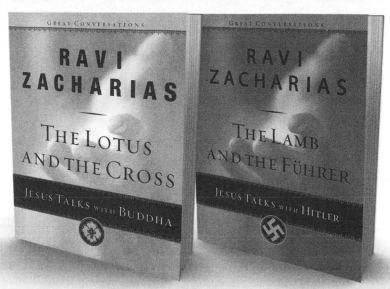